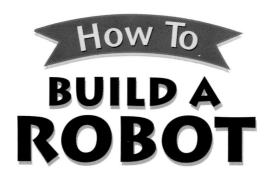

How To

BUILD A
ROBOT

How To

BUILD A
ROBOT

By CLIVE GIFFORD

Illustrated by
TIM BENTON

MUTTER
GRUMBLE!

FRANKLIN WATTS
A Division of Scholastic Inc.
New York Toronto London Auckland Sydney
Mexico City New Delhi Hong Kong
Danbury, Connecticut

First published 1999 by Oxford University Press
Great Clarendon Street, Oxford OX2 6DP

First American edition 2001 by Franklin Watts
A Division of Scholastic Inc.
90 Sherman Turnpike
Danbury, CT 06816

Catalog details are available from the Library of Congress
Cataloging-in-Publication Data

ISBN 0-531-14649-9 (lib. bdg.) 0-531-13997-2 (pbk.)

Printed in China

Contents

HOW TO BUILD A ROBOT

In 1997, a small six-wheeled robot decided all by itself to go right rather than left around a lump of rock. No big deal, you might think. But this robot, called *Sojourner*, made its decisions over 34 million miles (55 million kilometers) away—on Mars!

Sojourner is just one of the many amazing robots that have been built over the past forty years. Robots haven't been around long, but they have already swum underwater, flown through the air, and even played soccer. But it hasn't all been fun.

Robots have also worked long and hard in factories, helped save lives, crawled down deep mines, handled dangerously radioactive substances, and defused bombs.

All of this is only a start. Today, most of the world's robots are hidden away in factories and laboratories. But as further advances occur in computers—the machines that control robots and give them their ability to make decisions—robots are going to start hitting the streets.

In this book, you'll learn all about

☞ automation

☞ the development of robots

☞ robot parts and how they go together

☞ the different types of robots and what they can do

☞ what artificial intelligence is

☞ robots of the future

You'll also do experiments that will help you plan how to build your own super-smart robot.

CHAPTER ONE

WHAT IS A ROBOT, EXACTLY?

This is a tricky one. It's hard to say exactly what a robot is, because there are so many different kinds. But here's one definition:

> A robot is an automated machine that performs human-like actions and can be programmed to react to pre-recorded commands and, in some cases, react to certain external events.

Whaaat???!!

Quite a mouthful. Let's look at what it actually means.

"Automated" means that once it's been programmed, a robot can do its work without any help. Next comes the clever part—"programmed to react to pre-recorded commands." A robot can be programmed to do different jobs, just like a computer. This is what sets robots apart from most other machines. Most robots don't jump around between wildly different jobs—you don't see a robot arm handling delicate test tubes one minute and working in a coal mine the next. But, in theory, it could happen.

Now for the last part of the definition—"react to external events." Unlike most machines, robots can sense what is happening around them. They can also change what they are doing, depending on what their senses tell them. Which senses a robot has depends on the job it is designed to do. It may have cameras for "seeing," microphones for picking up sounds, and sensors for feeling pressure or heat. These senses give the robot information that will help it do its job.

Why Build Robots? ....

So now we know what robots are—versatile machines that can be told what to do and then left to get on with it. But why do we want to build robots? Well, why not? People have always fiddled with gadgets and machines. They can't help it. The human race is very curious about what it can make next, whether it's useful or not.

Some robots are built purely out of curiosity—to see if they can be made. But most robots are built because they are really useful and can do things other machines can't.

Advantage—Robots! ....

Industrial robots are expensive to make, but they can outperform humans in lots of ways. Robots don't get tired or bored doing the same simple task over and over. They don't need to go on vacation, take breaks for lunch, stop for a cup of tea, or go to the bathroom. And they don't mind nasty jobs like spray-painting cars or working with hot metals. All they need is a power source, an occasional maintenance break, and an annual overhaul.

Be a Robot Wizard
THINK YOU'RE BETTER
THAN A ROBOT?

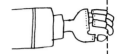

WHAT YOU'LL NEED
✚ a nut, bolt, or screw

WHAT TO DO
Try picking up a nut, bolt, or screw from one side of a table and placing it on the other side, again and again. Don't stop for a rest or to go to the bathroom—just keep going!

WHAT HAPPENS?
After five minutes, you'll be completely and utterly bored. After fifteen minutes (if you keep going that long), you'll probably be going nuts (or bolts). A robot will cheerfully do this job for 24 hours a day, 7 days a week, without ever considering going on strike.

YOU DON'T HAVE TO BE A ROBOT TO WORK HERE ...BUT IT HELPS!

KLUNK!

Robots can also be super-strong. A robot arm can lift ten times your body weight with ease.

But it's not all about strength. Robots can also perform delicate tasks on the tiniest scale. Robodoc is a robot that helps in hip-replacement operations. It drills a hole for the artificial hip to fit into the leg bone, and it does the job more accurately than any human surgeon. As a result, patients suffer less pain and are back on their feet sooner.

Be a Robot Wizard
DO YOU HAVE
A STEADY HAND?

Think all this fuss about robots being more accurate than you is nonsense? Try out this fun activity.

WHAT YOU'LL NEED
- a small electric buzzer
- tape
- some thick but bendable wire
- a battery
- modeling clay

WHAT TO DO
Bend a length of the wire into a wiggly shape and connect one end to the buzzer. Connect the other contact on the buzzer to the battery and hold the wire in place with some modeling clay.

Now attach another piece of wire to the other battery terminal and make a small loop about .5 inch (1cm) in diameter in its far end.

➤

Wrap some tape below the loop—this is where you will hold it. Hook it onto one end of the wiggly wire and try to guide the loop all the way to the other end without letting it touch the other wire and making the buzzer sound.

WHAT HAPPENS?
Tricky, eh?! It's really hard to get the loop from one end of the wire to the other without setting off the buzzer. But a robot arm that is properly programmed would never, ever cause the buzzer to sound.

To Boldly Go ....

Robots are strong, reliable, hardworking, and have very steady hands. But that's not all! Robots can also work in places where people can't. They can go almost anywhere—they aren't bothered by little things like blistering heat, freezing cold, or lack of air.

It must be cold. Even the robot's wearing a scarf!

One very important job that robots helped with was cleaning up after the nuclear reactor disaster at Chernobyl in the former Soviet Union. Robots were able to work in areas where the levels of radioactivity would have been deadly to humans.

Before you decide that robots are so perfect they make you sick, let's remind ourselves of an important limitation they have: their brains. Despite hundreds of years of research, robots are still pretty useless when it comes to making their own decisions.

We will look inside a robot's brain in Chapter 4. But first, let's look at the long chain of inventions and discoveries that led to today's robots.

CHAPTER TWO

THE LONG ROAD TO ROBOTS

The idea of robots has been around a lot longer than the real thing. All the way back in ancient Greek times, more than two thousand years ago, myths and legends told of human-like machines giving ordinary people a hard time. Take the legend of Talan, for example. He was a giant bronze figure who terrorized towns and villages by letting the sun reflect off his body to burn people alive.

Although the ancient Greeks made up plenty of stories about robots, they didn't get very far in building one. In fact, there was no real progress toward making a robot for hundreds of years. But then, in the fifth or sixth century in India...nothing happened!

A Big Fat Zero

India, fifth or sixth century A.D.

Here's the mathematician Vyas. He's just invented a new number—zero. You might think zero isn't very important, but try telling the difference between 10 and 1,000 without a zero! And without zero, the binary number system wouldn't work. Used by all computers to do their calculations, the binary system has only zeros and ones. Without zero, the computers we use to control robots wouldn't work.

19

Automata Matters

After the invention of zero, there wasn't much progress in robot development for quite a while. In the sixteenth century, the great artist Leonardo da Vinci sketched designs for parts of a robot in his notebooks, but no one knows if he ever actually built one. Then, in the eighteenth century, skilled clockmakers began to make realistic scale models of people and animals called automata. Some of them were pretty amazing.

The Master Model Maker

France, 1737

This is Jacques de Vaucanson, the most famous automaton-maker of his time. (Both automata were male, but we thought this made a nicer picture.)

The first figure de Vaucanson made was a clockwork flute player. When it was wound up, it blew through the instrument and pressed the keys. It could play eleven tunes. De Vaucanson's second figure was another musician. This one could play the flute with one hand while hitting a drum with the other. It could play twenty different tunes.

Now de Vaucanson is unveiling his third and greatest automaton— a clockwork duck! A duck? Yes, but what a duck! It is so convincing, it seems real. It swims around, quacks, and eats food. It even has droppings!

Other early automata could write a short letter or draw. But none of these machines were robots. Why not? Because automata are just wind-up dolls—they have a fixed set of actions, which they perform again and again. They can't vary them or respond to the world around them.

Revolutionary Machines ....

The skills involved in making complicated automata were used to make other machines in the eighteenth and nineteenth centuries. This was the time of the Industrial Revolution. Machines took over jobs such as spinning and weaving, which had previously been done by skilled craftspeople.

21

The steam engine, which had just been invented, provided a source of power for the new machines.

One of the most famous of the early machines was built by James Hargreaves.

Spinning a Yarn
Blackburn, England, 1764

Here's Jenny Hargreaves, daughter of weaver James Hargreaves. She's a smart girl, but a bit clumsy.

James noticed that the spindle on Jenny's overturned spinning wheel still worked when it was upright. He realized that a whole set of upright spindles could be turned by one machine.

Hmmm, that gives me an idea!

Hargreaves eventually built a machine that could spin eighty threads at the same time. He called it the spinning jenny, after his daughter.

The spinning jenny wasn't automatic—it needed people to control it. But soon people invented controllers that could run a machine by themselves, at least in part. One type of controller was the flyball governor, invented by Scottish engineer James Watt.

Watt's flyball governor! It was used on steam engines to keep them from going too fast.

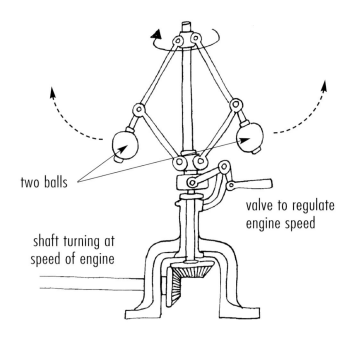

two balls

valve to regulate engine speed

shaft turning at speed of engine

The balls on Watt's governor were thrown farther out the faster the engine shaft spun. They were connected to a valve that controlled the amount of steam reaching the engine. The farther out the balls moved, the less steam was allowed into the engine.

The governor was special because it was one of the first devices to have feedback. Feedback is when information about the machine is "fed back" to a controlling device, which makes adjustments to how the machine is working. Robots and other automated machines rely on feedback to do their jobs.

Your body uses feedback, too. It happens so naturally, you are not aware of it. Think about turning on the microwave. As you reach for the "start" button, your eyes send constant feedback signals to your brain. These tell the brain how far your hand has moved and how close it is to the button. Your brain uses this feedback to adjust the movement of your hand until—presto—you're right on the button.

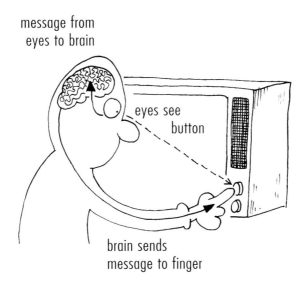

message from
eyes to brain

eyes see
button

brain sends
message to finger

Want to see how feedback of different types helps you? Try this experiment.

Be a Robot Wizard
FEEDBACK FINGER

WHAT YOU'LL NEED
✤ a marble or other playing piece
✤ a pegboard or something else with regular holes, such as a Chinese checkers board

WHAT TO DO
Rest the marble on the pegboard a certain number of holes away from the edge. Close your eyes and move an outstretched finger forward until you think it's directly above the marble. Open your eyes. How close are you?

5, 6, 7...!

Now try again, but this time run your finger along the board, feeling the holes. Open your eyes when you think your fingertip is on the hole next to the marble.

WHAT HAPPENED?
The first time, your finger was probably close to the marble, but not right over it. You can't be really accurate, because your brain isn't getting any feedback. The second time, your finger should end up alongside the marble, because the brain is getting feedback from the touch sensors in your fingertip.

Punching Programs...................

Another important piece of robot technology came along in the nineteenth century: the first programmable machines. Early programs weren't made for computers; they were for looms.

Automation Looming
France, 1804

Joseph-Marie Jacquard had the idea for a new invention in 1790. But he didn't get far with his idea because of a small distraction—the French Revolution.

I can't think straight!

BOOM!

BOOM!

CHEER!

AARGH!

But by 1804, Jacquard had managed to build his invention, a loom for weaving cloth. It used stiff cards punched with holes to tell the loom which colored threads to weave and where. Different punched cards created different patterns. Apart from making it possible to weave complicated patterns with ease—and making Jacquard wildly rich—the loom was the world's first programmable machine.

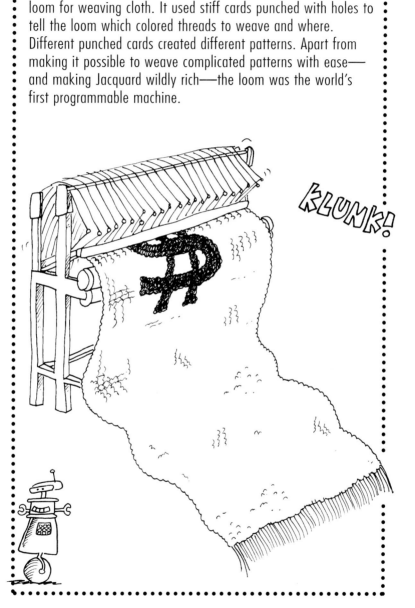

Punched cards were used for programming machines throughout the nineteenth century. Then, in 1890, an American named Herman Hollerith built an electric machine that used punched cards to hold information as well as instructions. His machine won a competition to complete part of the U.S. census in the shortest time. The other contestants averaged over 50 hours for the test. Hollerith's machine took just 5 hours.

Hollerith set up the Tabulating Machine Company to make his punched card machines. His company later became the International Business Machines Corporation—IBM to you and me.

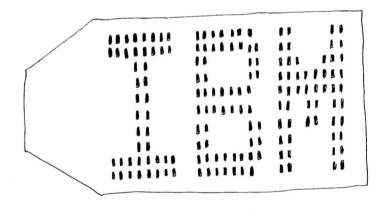

In England, another man had made a machine that was much more than just a calculator. His name was Charles Babbage.

Making a Difference
England, nineteenth century

Charles Babbage was the first man to design and build a fully working computer—well, most of one. Between 1822 and 1835, he developed something called a Difference Engine, designed to calculate tables of mathematical figures very accurately. Then he moved on to a much more ambitious machine—the Analytical Engine. This had most of the features of a modern computer.

There was one snag with Babbage's Analytical Engine: no one could build it! It had to use wheels and cogs rather than electronic circuits, because electrically powered machines hadn't been invented yet. Even the best engineers of the time couldn't build a machine accurate enough to work properly.

Making an Exhibition of Themselves........

With the discovery and use of electricity in the early twentieth century, automata made a bit of a comeback. At fairs and exhibitions in the 1920s and 1930s, people were amazed to see life-sized metal machines that seemed to perform basic human actions and even respond to voice commands.

These electrically powered machines were still automata—they had no ability to think for themselves. The hundreds of realistic mechanical dinosaurs and aliens now used in films are the modern equivalents of automata. These remote-controlled devices are called animatronics. They look incredibly real, but everything they do has to be controlled by a human.

Robots Rule the World................................

The word "robot" was first used in the 1920s, not by a scientist or an inventor but by a Czech playwright named Karel Capek. Capek made up the word for his play *RUR (Rossum's Universal Robots)*. His robots started out working hard, but then they turned against their human masters and eventually took over the world.

Since then, robots in science-fiction books and films have often been shown as powerful, evil creatures with only one aim—WORLD DOMINATION!

Don't worry, this couldn't really happen. First of all, real-life robots can't do more than they are programmed to. Lots of them can't even move—they are fixed in one place. And even those that can move around wouldn't have the battery power to manage world domination.

The Invention of the Transistor ....

The first computers were made in the 1940s. They relied on switches called vacuum tubes to make decisions and perform calculations. They were large, cumbersome, and unreliable. The ENIAC computer had about nineteen thousand tubes, and at least one broke every two minutes!

All this changed with the transistor, invented by three Americans named Walter Brattain, John Bardeen, and William Shockley. Transistors, which control the flow of electricity in the machines, work much faster than tubes, and they don't break down as often. From the 1950s on, computers were made by linking thousands of transistors together.

It wasn't long after transistors made an appearance that the first working robot was invented.

33

What a Great Party
United States, 1956

Inventor George Devol and a young aerospace engineer named Joseph Engelberger have just met at a cocktail party. Over drinks and snacks, they talk about Devol's patent for a moving arm that can unload boxes according to instructions held on a magnetic drum.

The drum can be re-recorded to make the arm move in a different way.

In the years after the party, the two men produce the first industrial robot. It is called Unimate. The first Unimate is put to work in a car factory in 1961.

Chips with Everything ....

Transistors were soon replaced by something even smaller—silicon chips. One tiny chip of silicon could carry the equivalent of thousands of transistors, connected to make a complicated electronic circuit. It wasn't long before the computer's whole central processing unit (its "brain") could be fitted onto a single chip. This was the first microprocessor.

Modern microprocessors allow computers to make lots of small decisions very quickly. Inside a microprocessor, thousands and thousands of switches are arranged into circuits called logic gates. These help the computer make decisions by only letting electricity pass if certain conditions are met.

Be a Robot Wizard
MAKE A SIMPLE LOGIC GATE

WHAT YOU'LL NEED
- ✦ a flashlight battery
- ✦ a flashlight bulb
- ✦ electrical wire
- ✦ four thumbtacks
- ✦ two small pieces of wood
- ✦ two metal paper clips

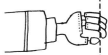

WHAT TO DO
Arrange the items as shown in the picture (next page). Turn on one of the switches by moving the paper clip to touch the second thumbtack. Try turning on the other switch, then both switches. ➤

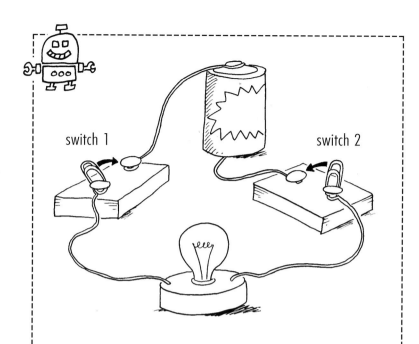

switch 1

switch 2

WHAT HAPPENS?

What you have made is an AND logic gate. Electricity will only pass through the circuit and light the bulb if both switch 1 AND switch 2 are on.

CHAPTER THREE

ROBOT PARTS

Let's take a closer look at the various parts of a robot and how they work:

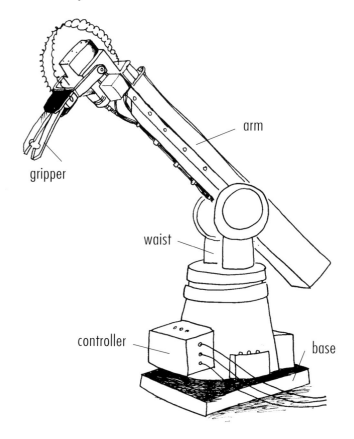

This is the most common type of robot—the robot arm. No legs, no head, no body, just a single arm. (There is a waist, though.)

Robot arms have joints, just like human arms. The different directions in which a joint can move are called degrees of freedom. Most robot arms have five or six degrees of freedom.

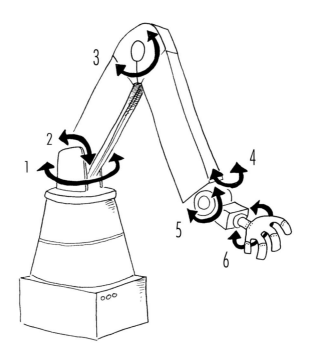

Power Plays ....

You need power to get a robot moving. Some robot arms use electric motors for muscles, but there are other types of power. Robots that have lots of heavy lifting to do use hydraulic power. Hydraulics uses liquids in cylinders to produce lots of force. Other robots use air power—pneumatics. Pneumatic robots aren't as strong as hydraulic ones, but they can react much faster.

38

Hydraulics and pneumatics are handy in situations where a stray spark from an electric motor could cause a fire or explosion—for instance, checking gas leaks in tanks or pipelines.

Be a Robot Wizard
PNEUMATIC POWER IN ACTION

WHAT YOU'LL NEED
- ❖ a balloon
- ❖ a heavy book
- ❖ an elastic band
- ❖ a bicycle pump

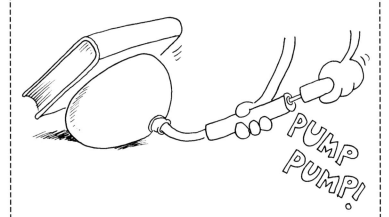

PUMP PUMP!

WHAT TO DO
Slip the connector of the bicycle pump into the mouth of the balloon, and fasten it on tightly with the elastic band. Put the balloon underneath the book, leaving the end with the pump attached sticking out. Now pump air into the balloon.

WHAT HAPPENS?
As you blow the balloon up, the book is lifted.

If you have an air mattress and a foot pump, you could try lifting an adult with air power. Get the person to lie on the mattress, then use the foot pump to blow it up.

The End of the Matter.........................

The business end of a robot arm is called an actuator. Catchy name, eh? Let's call it a hand instead. The hand is the part that does all the work, from spray-painting car body panels to defusing bombs. Robot arms can be fitted with different hands to perform jobs such as drilling, grinding, and riveting. Pretty handy!

Gripping Stuff ....

Most robot arms come with an actuator called a gripper, which is used for—you guessed it—gripping things. Grippers are built for handling one or two types of objects. But no gripper can compete with the human hand when it comes to handling lots of different things.

Why is your hand so good at gripping? Well, your brain and hand work together to automatically adjust the amount of force needed to grip a particular object. Think how hard you grip a climbing rope in gym class, and how lightly you hold a delicate flower.

It's not easy to program a robot to use the right amount of force to grip something.

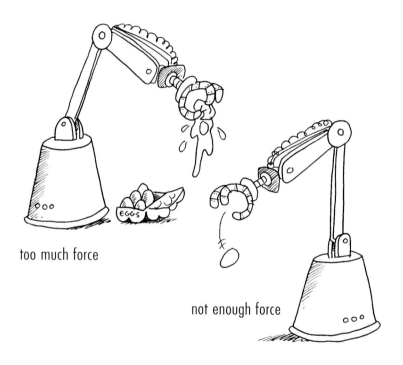

too much force

not enough force

Some robots get around the tricky business of holding objects by using a different type of gripper altogether. For example, robots that handle iron and steel can use electromagnets—magnets that can be turned on and off by electricity.

42

Be a Robot Wizard
MAKE AN ELECTROMAGNET

WHAT YOU'LL NEED

- ❖ a flashlight battery
- ❖ 3 feet (1 m) of electrical wire
- ❖ duct tape
- ❖ a large iron nail
- ❖ some metal paper clips

WHAT TO DO

Wind most of the wire tightly around the nail. Strip off the plastic covering from the last inch or so of both ends of the wire, and use tape to attach one wire to the top of the battery. Touch the other end of the wire to the bottom of the battery. Hold the paper clips near the wire.

WHAT HAPPENS?

Your electromagnet can now grip metal paper clips. Remove the wire from the battery, and the paper clips will drop.

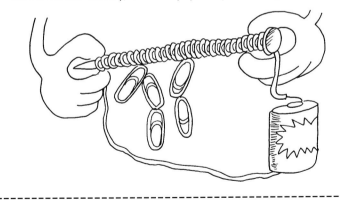

Some robots use powerful vacuum suckers as grippers. Vacuum suckers can pick up and handle large sheets of metal, glass, or plastic.

Be a Robot Wizard
SUCK IT AND SEE

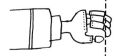

WHAT YOU'LL NEED
- ❖ a small sheet of paper
- ❖ a drinking straw
- ❖ your mouth

WHAT TO DO
Put one end of the straw in your mouth, and press the other end against the piece of paper. Suck hard through the straw.

WHAT HAPPENS?
The paper "sticks" to the straw! If you keep sucking, you should be able to lift the paper off the table.

Vacuum suckers on robots work in much the same way.

On the Move...

Robot arms in factories tend to be fixed in place, but some robots need to be able to move around. Tracks, wheels, and legs are the main methods for moving robots across land. Each has its good and bad points.

Tracks

ADVANTAGES
Good over bumpy ground. Rugged and reliable. Good at climbing stairs.

DISADVANTAGES
Very slow to move.

DUM DE DUM!

USES
On the surface of the moon and other planets; for bomb-disposal robots.

EXAMPLE
Bomb-disposal robots are often tracked robots fitted with an extending robot arm. Different tools can be attached to the arm to, for example, unlock a car door. One tool, called a disrupter, can actually defuse a bomb with a powerful jet of water.

Wheels

ADVANTAGES

Fastest movers of the three types.

DISADVANTAGES

Not so good on rough or uneven ground.

TINY PEBBLES

USES

In factories to carry materials around, in hospitals to carry medical supplies.

EXAMPLE

Automatic guided vehicles (or AGVs for short) follow a set path as they transport objects around a factory, office, or hospital. The path is often marked out by an electrical cable buried in the floor. Some AGVs can even use elevators.

Four or More Legs

ADVANTAGES

Great for climbing over obstacles.

DISADVANTAGES

Most complicated design; difficult to build.

USES

At disaster sites, across unpredictable ground, in power stations.

EXAMPLE

Robug III is an eight-legged research robot designed to travel over difficult terrain. It weighs 130 lbs. and can transport loads of up to 220 lbs. up walls, as well as along the ground.

This robot's driving me up the wall!

It's very important for a robot to stay upright, because once it tips over, it can't always get back up again. Tracked, wheeled, and multi-leg robots are therefore built with many points of contact with the ground.

Humans have only two legs. Why not robots? Because two legs aren't the most stable system around. We don't fall over when we walk because we have an incredibly advanced balancing system. But it's much harder to put a robot on two legs. You can see why in this next experiment.

Be a Robot Wizard
FOUR LEGS GOOD, TWO LEGS BAD

WHAT YOU'LL NEED
✦ a toy doll or action figure with movable arms and legs

WHAT TO DO
1. Stand the doll upright.
2. Lift one of the doll's legs up and forward, as if it is taking a step. Let go.

➤

3. Now try putting the doll on its hands and knees (or feet, if your doll can't bend at the knees). Lift one arm up and forward as if the doll were about to crawl.

WHAT HAPPENS?
In the upright position, the doll has only one point of contact once it lifts a leg. This is very unstable, and the doll will most likely fall over. But on hands and knees, the doll still has three points of contact with the ground after lifting one arm. This is much more stable.

Two-legged, human-like robots may not be that far away, however. A team of scientists in Japan have built *P3*, a two-legged robot about the size of a small human. Sensors in its feet and stomach send messages to *P3's* computer brain to help it stay upright. *P3* can walk over rough ground and even up and down stairs.

Flying Robots ....

Not all robots are stuck on the ground. Some of them can fly!

Cypher is a flying robot. It looks a bit like a UFO and can zoom through the air, then stop and hover. It is designed for spying and taking aerial photos.

50

Cypher is designed for spying up close. *Global Hawk* is a flying robot designed for spying from much farther away. It can fly over 13,700 miles (22,000 km) in one trip. To avoid detection, it operates at twice the altitude of a passenger airliner. Its slender body is packed with powerful zoom cameras, and a 13-foot (4-m)-wide satellite dish in its nose can send back top-secret pictures in an instant. Mission planners instruct *Global Hawk* roughly where to go and what to look for, but the robot does the rest itself. That includes avoiding bad weather and flying in complex patterns to make it difficult to be picked up on radar.

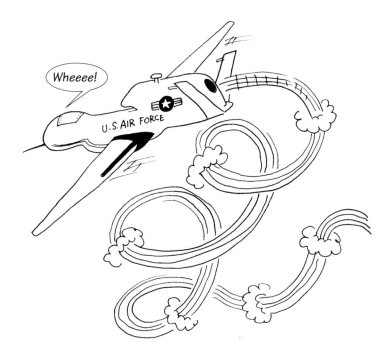

Robots out in space can fly without wings or powerful engines. NASA's robot camera AERCam Sprint is shaped like a soccer ball. It can whiz around in space, sending back incredible views of the space shuttle or a space station.

Similar free-flying robot balls may soon be with us on Earth. Fitted with more powerful mini-jets to keep them in the air, they would be very handy for high-rise views when building skyscrapers. They could even replace helicopters that fly over roads to check traffic conditions.

Underwater Robots............................

Other robots travel underwater. Underwater robots
don't have to be built to resist water pressure, and
they don't need large supplies of air, food, and water
since they don't have a crew. This means they can go
deeper underwater and stay there for longer.

Underwater robots are already used for monitoring
pipelines and cables on the seabed, mapping the
ocean floor, and salvaging wrecks. For example, the
robot *Jason Jr.* traveled to a depth of 13,000 feet
(3,965 m) to explore and photograph the wreck of the
ocean liner *Titanic*.

Be a Robot Wizard
SEE HOW WATER PRESSURE INCREASES WITH DEPTH

WHAT YOU'LL NEED
- some modeling clay
- a large can
- something for making small holes in the can (have an adult help you with this part)

WHAT TO DO
Make three holes in the can: one near the bottom, one in the middle, and one near the top. Plug the holes with modeling clay from the outside and fill the can up over a sink or in a bathtub. Now remove the clay from the holes.

WHAT HAPPENS?
Water runs out of the holes, of course. But look at how far the water shoots out from each hole. It shoots out farther from the hole at the bottom than it does from the hole at the top. That's because at the bottom hole, the water is under more pressure than at the top hole. The more water above, the greater the pressure.

CHAPTER FOUR

ROBOT CONTROL

Without instructions, a robot is one dumb machine. So how do we tell robots what to do?

Jason Jr. is a remote-controlled robot. This means it is linked by a cable or through radio signals to a human controller some distance away. Some say robots controlled by a human operator from a distance aren't really robots at all. But most of these remote-controlled machines can actually do some things for themselves. For example, a robot might be told by a human to move to a particular place, but the robot has to figure out the route for itself.

55

Some robot arms in factories are physically taken through their moves by a human operator. Each movement of the arm is recorded in the robot's memory, so that the robot can repeat the whole set of moves over and over again.

Computer programs are collections of instructions. At the heart of a modern robot controller are microprocessors made of silicon chips. The robot's controller can run computer programs itself, or it can get instructions from a program running on a separate computer.

Making Sense ....

Sensors are a crucial part of most robots. They provide feedback to its controller, just as your senses send information to your brain.

Sensors help a robot figure out where all its parts are, where it is going, and what is happening around it. We take it for granted that we know what our body parts are doing, but a robot doesn't have a clue—not without sensors to tell its controller, anyway.

Many robots have sensors that use different strengths of electrical signals to represent distances. To see how this works, try the following experiment.

Be a Robot Wizard
MAKE A POTENTIOMETER

WHAT YOU'LL NEED
- ❖ a battery
- ❖ a bulb in a bulb holder
- ❖ three pieces of electrical wire
- ❖ duct tape
- ❖ a wooden pencil split open to reveal its lead

WHAT TO DO
Attach one wire from the battery to the bulb. Attach another wire from the battery to one end of the pencil lead, and the third wire from the other end of the pencil lead to the bulb.

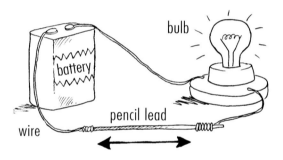

Now slide one of the wires touching the pencil lead closer to the other wire. Slide it away again.

WHAT HAPPENS?
Moving the wires closer together causes the bulb to shine more brightly. Moving the wire away causes it to dim. Why? Pencil lead resists the flow of electricity. The more pencil lead in the circuit, the less electricity reaches the bulb. Potentiometers used in robots work in a similar way—the position of a part of a robot can be represented by an electrical signal that changes as the part moves.

For a mobile robot, it's not enough to know where all its parts are. It needs to know what's around it. So it uses proximity sensors to measure how far away objects are. Proximity sensors work like radar, or like a bat's echolocation system. The sensor sends out a sound or light signal and measures the time it takes for the signal to bounce back from whatever it hits. The farther away an object is, the longer it will take for the signal to bounce back.

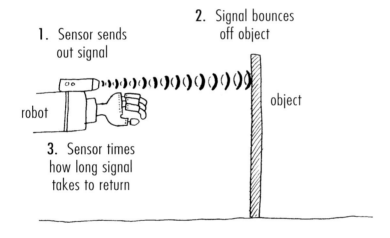

2. Signal bounces off object

1. Sensor sends out signal

object

robot

3. Sensor times how long signal takes to return

Proximity sensors aren't the only way a robot can get information about its surroundings. Some robot sensors check out the temperature, the amount of light, or the presence of particular gases or chemicals. Robot "sniffers," for example, can detect a leaking gas or chemical pipe.

Some robots have a limited sort of vision, using video cameras. The robot scans the video pictures, looking for objects it has been taught to recognize or things that are moving. Robots need complex computer programs to make sense of the images they "see." Even then, their "eyes" can easily be fooled.

Our eyes and brain make up a much more powerful vision package than any robot has. But even we can be fooled, as this optical illusion shows.

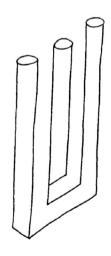

Have a close look at the image on page 60. It drives your eyes crazy! That's because your brain is trying to make a three-dimensional image out of a flat, two-dimensional one.

Out and About ....

The need to "see" becomes particularly important when robots are designed to go out and about. It's easier for a robot to move around on the flat, smooth floor of a science lab or factory; it can be much harder to negotiate the ups and downs of a garden or a golf course. Two handy robots, a lawn mower and a golf bag carrier, have found different ways to get around outdoors.

Robomower uses a guide wire, pinned around the edge of the lawn, as a boundary fence. It won't travel past the wire. Robomower also has proximity sensors to detect obstacles on the lawn—anything from a ball to a garden statue.

Its proximity sensors have gone wrong again!

The Intelecaddy robot golf bag carrier has a more complicated system. It has an entire map of the golf course—every hole, bunker, mound, and dip—mapped into its memory. A global positioning system lets the robot know exactly where it is all the time, so it can automatically steer clear of bunkers and water hazards. It follows its owner using a tiny radio beeper worn on the golfer's waist.

Thinking Robots

We've seen how robots can be used to do difficult, dangerous, or boring jobs. But even the most sophisticated of these robots is still a machine that can only do exactly what it has been programmed for, and no more. The real challenge is to make a robot that can learn and think for itself.

CHAPTER FIVE

ARTIFICIAL INTELLIGENCE

What's artificial intelligence? Glad you asked. There are two sides to AI (the abbreviation for artificial intelligence). It's partly about studying human and animal brains to figure out how they work. The other part of AI is about trying to use what we know about our brains to improve the thinking ability of robots, computers, and other machines.

Humans and animals make decisions based on their experience, by either instinct or intuition. AI is about trying to understand how we do this, then trying to program machines to work the same way.

One thing is for certain: AI is a tough subject. There are lots of areas to study. To be well-versed in AI, you've got to know something about everything.

Because there are so many subjects to learn about, people who study AI usually get together in teams.

You're Amazing!...............................

AI scientists have a difficult job because they're trying to compete with something really amazing—you!

I'm glad you recognize my genius.

Well, not just you. Your friends and relatives, too. In fact, any human—even your teachers!

Are teachers human?

We all have bodies chock-full of sophisticated sensors linked to an amazingly powerful controller—your brain. Machines are still a long way behind people when it comes to understanding information and acting on it. The human brain handles masses of information, just like a computer, but it does much more. It can handle many types of information at the same time, sift through everything, pick out the

64

important parts, learn from them, and then make complex decisions. Robots and computers simply aren't in the same league (not yet, anyway).

Brain Works ....

So what is it about our brains that makes them so smart? Although scientists still don't totally understand how the brain works, they have some idea of how complex the brain is.

Your brain is the control center for your whole body. It has a communication network of many thousands of messenger cells, called nerves, which send information into the brain from your senses and carry instructions from the brain to other parts of the body. Nerves send information as pulses of electricity along nerve fibers. These electric pulses are "all or nothing": a nerve either fires, or it doesn't.

The brain is made up of lots of nerve cells called neurons. Each neuron is connected to lots of others—about a thousand on average. But these connections are one-way—they are inputs, not outputs. So a neuron gets information from lots of other neurons, but it can only send out one signal of its own.

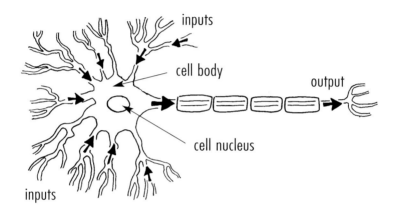

One of the things that makes the brain so powerful is the sheer number of these neurons. There are a staggering 100 billion of them in a human brain. Since each neuron is connected to 1,000 others, that makes a total of about 100 trillion nerve connections!

Intelligence Test.................................

Since the human brain is so amazing, one very good test of a machine's artificial intelligence is how well it can imitate a human. This is something that Alan Turing, one of the pioneers of AI, proposed in 1950.

The Turing Test

This is Alan Turing.

Hi!

During World War II, Turing worked on the top-secret computers that deciphered the Germans' most fiendish war code, Enigma. Now he's interested in artificial intelligence, and he has devised a test for determining just how smart a computer really is.

So how does the Turing test work? Easy as A, B, C.

A computer is set up in one room, and a human judge sits in another. The judge "talks" to the computer through a monitor and keyboard.

Sometimes another human takes control of the computer in the sealed room and has a conversation with the judge. At other times the computer itself answers.

The test is: can the human judge tell the difference between a human answering him and a computer?

➤

- Hi, I'm Sam, what's your name?

- OptiFlex GX4000... oops, no, it's, uh... Gary.

Some computer programs don't do too well, but there are computer programs that can make a computer respond very much like a human. So far, no computer has been able to fool a human judge for long. But they can hold some pretty interesting conversations! Here's just a part of one...

Program: *Hello. My name is Jim. Who are you?*
Judge: Charles.
Program: *Charles is a wrestler in* As You Like It.
Charles is the King of France in King Henry VI, Part I.
Judge: Do you like Shakespeare?
Program: *Yeah, sure.*
Judge: What do you like about his plays?
Program: *Well, there's a certain* je ne sais quoi.
Judge: I think it is great that you like his plays.
Program: *I like phasers.*
Judge: Do you mean like those in *Star Trek*?
Program: *It's possible.*
Judge: What's possible?
Program: *Nothing.*

Super Model! ....

Scientists have found several different ways of building machines with AI potential. One method is called the top-down, or model, approach. This involves getting a computer to decide what to do by comparing what it is experiencing with a model of the real world in its memory. The model is usually of only a very narrow slice of the real world—lots of information about playing chess, for example, or about the symptoms of common illnesses. No robot or computer has yet been built with a wide knowledge base like ours. But in their particular fields, some of these top-down computers can outperform humans.

Blue and Bluer
New York, 1996

This is the Deep Blue computer program. It's pretty good at chess. It has been programmed with all the most famous chess games of the past, and it can look at 500 million different chess moves in one second. Deep Blue has beaten some of the best human chess players in the world. Now it's up against World Chess Champion Garry Kasparov. Despite Deep Blue's awesome power, Kasparov bamboozles the computer and wins the match. ➤

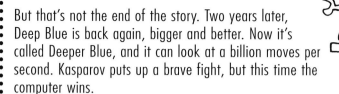

But that's not the end of the story. Two years later, Deep Blue is back again, bigger and better. Now it's called Deeper Blue, and it can look at a billion moves per second. Kasparov puts up a brave fight, but this time the computer wins.

Bottoms Up! ....

The top-down approach works well in a few very limited cases. But it's not much good when it comes to programming free-moving robots in an ever-changing world. The bottom-up, or behavioral, approach is more promising. It's based on giving a machine a set of basic rules on how to behave, plus the ability to learn and add to those rules based on its experience of the real world. Over time, these kinds of learning programs can build up a machine's knowledge.

70

One type of bottom-up program is the neural network. This imitates the workings of a small part of the brain. A neural network is made up of a number of nodes, each of which acts like a neuron in the brain.

Like neurons, a node gets signals from many other nodes, but sends out only one signal of its own. And like the brain, a neural network can "learn." For example, neural nets are good at recognizing patterns, such as letters or numbers. A neural network that has been programmed to recognize handwritten words is at first not very good at it—it may have trouble reading some people's handwriting, or it may misread some words.

But as the network is trained with lots of different handwriting samples, it gets much better at "reading."

Some neural networks can even come up with ideas of their own. One scientist built a neural network and programmed it with the tunes of some popular songs. He then set it to work to create tunes of its own. It came up with over eleven thousand new tunes!

Learning to Survive.............................

In living creatures, parents reproduce and pass on their characteristics to the next generation through genes. In each generation, the most successful individuals survive and produce young. The less successful ones don't produce young. This is the process of natural selection, the driving force of evolution. Some AI researchers have used a kind of natural selection process to produce programs that "evolve."

Robot Breeding
England, 1995

A group of thirty robots has learned to spot a white triangle against a black background. Easy enough, except that no human wrote the program that controls the robots. Instead, the robots were programmed with a random mix of instructions. This random mix was then tested to see how well the different programs did with the task of recognizing a white triangle. The programs that came closest to working were kept, while the others were thrown away.

So what's so special about this triangle?

The programs that survived the "first generation" were then mixed and duplicated to produce a "second generation." These new programs were again tested, and the best were kept to make a "third generation," then a fourth, and so on. (This kind of program is called a genetic algorithm.) By the thirtieth generation, a program that could make a robot move toward the white triangle and stop in front of it had "evolved."

It's possible that scientists using this approach will be able to evolve programs that allow a robot to work in a wide range of situations.

Feeling Fuzzy ....

A computer works with digital information coursing through millions of switches that are either on or off, 1 or 0. This encourages black-and-white, true-or-false thinking, but the real world is rarely that simple. Fuzzy logic is all about using special programming to include a range of values, not just 1 or 0. This allows notions such as "relatively warm" or "a very sharp bend in the road" to be computed. It is an attempt to apply a more human-like way of thinking to computer programming. Fuzzy logic is already being used in everyday devices such as washing machines and the latest car controls.

Working Together ....

So far, we have looked at ways of making individual robots intelligent. Another idea is to get robots with different abilities to work together. For example, a group of robots working together in a building would be able to come up with a picture of the inside.

Robot Soccer ....

It's no joke—robot researchers all around the world are putting together soccer teams! Soccer is a good way to test many different aspects of robot research. The robots have to have a good sensory system to know where the ball is; the ability to move quickly on the field, without bumping into other players; and the ability to work together as a team to score goals.

There are lots of different robot soccer competitions. Most are between small wheeled robots, but researchers are working on full-sized robot soccer players. There are even junior robot soccer competitions, where children can program pre-built robots made of plastic building bricks and then have them play against each other.

Robot soccer games have to be short, because the robots can't carry enough battery power to keep going for long periods. But there's plenty of excitement—in one 10-minute game, the score was 20-0!

Robot soccer is still in its infancy. But the organizers of RoboCup, one of the robot soccer competitions, dream big. By 2050, they aim to build a team of humanlike robot soccer players that can take on the reigning human world champions—and beat them.

CHAPTER SIX

TIME TO MAKE THAT HIGH-IQ ROBOT

Well done! If you've gotten this far, you've learned enough to start planning your own high-IQ robot. First, you need to decide what you want your robot to do, and where. Your decisions will affect how you put your wonder machine together.

Ask yourself some questions. What do you want your robot to do? And what features will it need to do those things?

Where will you want to use your robot—indoors or outdoors? If outdoors, it will need a waterproof covering.

Getting Around ....

For your robot to be most effective, it will need to be mobile. You'll have to choose how it will move around. A tracked set of wheels that can turn and tilt to go up stairs would be handy for indoors.

Another way of solving the stairs problem is to make a bouncing robot. A group of robot researchers in the United States is working on a small rolling robot, about the size and shape of a toilet-paper roll, which has a spring-loaded leg to help it jump up stairs.

How Big? ....

What size will your robot be? If it's an indoor robot, it will have to fit through doors, and if it's too tall it might tip over. On the other hand, if it's too small, it won't be able to lift anything heavy. A search-and-rescue robot being developed in the United States has come up with a smart answer to the size problem. The main robot is 6.5 feet (2 m) long, and is designed for climbing over rubble in disaster areas. But it carries a much smaller, tracked robot that can be used to explore tight places.

A squat shape would be the most stable for your robot —but will it be able to reach everything you want it to work with? Try this experiment to help you decide.

Be a Robot Wizard
ROBOT REACH 1

Turn yourself into a robot and see how far you can reach with a straight robot arm versus one with a middle joint.

WHAT TO DO
Kneel down with one of your arms straight out in front of you. You are now a typical-sized personal home robot. Start shuffling around the room on your knees. See what you can reach with your arm rigid and only able to move up and down. Now try reaching for the same things, but allow your elbow to bend.

WHAT HAPPENS?
Shuffling around on your knees is pretty slow, but it's typical robot speed. Do you find a number of things out of reach? Bet you do. Once you let your arm bend at the elbow, things should get easier. You should be able to reach a few more items.

What about the things that are out of reach, even for a jointed arm? Will you modify your house or give the robot a telescopic arm that can extend upward? Remember, the longer the arm, the less weight it can carry and the harder it is to control, as the next experiment shows.

BISCUITS

NUTS + BOLTS

I wish
I'd been designed with
telescopic arms!

81

Be a Robot Wizard
ROBOT REACH 2

WHAT YOU'LL NEED
- ✤ a fishing pole (or any long stick)
- ✤ a piece of string
- ✤ a magnet
- ✤ paper clips

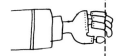

WHAT TO DO
Tie the magnet to the string, and tie the string to one end of the pole so that the magnet dangles 12-20 inches (30-50 centimeters) below the pole. Now place a couple of metal paper clips on the floor a few inches apart and identify the one you want to pick up with the magnet. First, try holding the pole a short way away from the string. Then try holding the pole at the end opposite to the magnet.

WHAT HAPPENS?
When you hold the pole up close to the magnet, it's pretty easy to pick up the paper clip you're after. But when you hold the pole at the end farthest from the magnet, it's much harder to control it accurately.

Sensor Situation ....

Once you've got the size right, it's time to think about sensors. You'll want your robot to be packed with sensors of many different kinds. It will need proximity sensors to keep it from bumping into things. You might also want temperature sensors so that your robot can sound the alarm in case of fire. A video-based vision system will probably be best for your robot's main sensors. Linked up to advanced software, your robot will be able to judge objects and distances.

Where you place the camera or cameras is important. If you put a camera on the robot's arm, it can send back visual signals of places the camera on the body can't see.

Your high-IQ robot should have its sensors concentrated in the places where it needs them most. Your body is designed this way, as this next experiment shows.

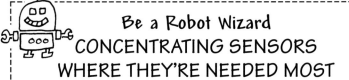

Be a Robot Wizard
CONCENTRATING SENSORS
WHERE THEY'RE NEEDED MOST

WHAT YOU'LL NEED
- ✤ a blindfold
- ✤ a friend
- ✤ two pencils

WHAT TO DO
Put on the blindfold. Now ask your friend to touch you lightly on your arms, legs, hands, fingers, and back, sometimes using one pencil point, sometimes using two. Say whether you can feel one point or two.

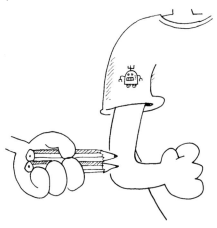

WHAT HAPPENS?
The places you get right most often are the places where your body has the most touch sensors, such as your fingers. Your body has been carefully designed so that the information-collectors are put where they're needed most. In places such as your back, there are many fewer touch sensors.

Command Center ....

Next, you need to think about how you are going to control your robot. How many kinds of input will you give it? Voice commands are easy, so try attaching a voice-activated system. It will need special devices called filters to cut out background noise. You might want to add a program to teach the robot to recognize your voice, so that it only responds to instructions from you. You could also attach a scanner so that the robot can "read" words on a piece of paper.

Make sure to make your commands clear. For example, if you write "1 Burn Gardens," is this the first line of an address or the first of a numbered list of instructions?

If you don't program in some foolproof mechanism, you could be sorry!

Great Brains ....

Now, the tricky part. You'll need a stack of clever software all working together to give your robot the ability to act on its own in response to the tasks you give it. You'll want to give it the ability to react to the most common situations, so you might choose to supply it with a knowledge base—rules to work by.

Jasper = B for Bully.
IF B knocks on door THEN
[activate voice box]
SAY Data 1
Data 1: "Not in.
Has left the country."

You will probably also want to include a learning program, based on neural networks or learning software, so that your robot can learn from its experiences and build up its knowledge.

You might also want to build in some fuzzy logic, because your intelligent robot pal could encounter situations that aren't black and white.

86

Connections...

Giving your robot access to a computer network could make it much more useful. Your robot's powerful onboard computer might well interact with the Internet in the future. But how will it connect to the network? Perhaps, like R2D2 in the movie *Star Wars*, it will use a probe to physically connect to a socket. Better still, it could use radio signals to keep in touch with the network.

By the way, don't forget to fit rubber bumpers around the edges of your robot. This will soften the blow if your robot accidentally crashes into the walls, the furniture, or the cat.

Building Your Robot ....

With the planning completed, you can go shopping!

Obviously, it will take some time to put the machine together...

...but if you get there, you'll have a super-powerful, amazing machine at your disposal.

CHAPTER SEVEN

ROBOTS IN THE FUTURE

So, you've got your intelligent robot—what are you going to do with it? Put your feet up and let it do all the household chores? It's great to let machines do all the work. But what else? How about getting it to help with your homework? It could surf the Internet while you're out and present the key facts to you when you get back. Cyber-tastic!

Robots are unlikely to replace human teachers in the classroom. But robotic tutors may enter our homes in the next twenty years or so, whether you build one or not. Robots may come with a database and onboard dictionary so they can spell, explain difficult words, and answer all your questions.

In fact, the hardest tasks for a robot will continue to be some of the things people find very easy, such as recognizing and greeting another person or making an impromptu snack out of what's available in the refrigerator and kitchen cupboards.

This is because robots, even intelligent models of the future, will find it hard to build up the general knowledge people have in so many different areas.

On the Farm

Farming is tiring, back-breaking work—ideally suited to intelligent machines built to withstand all that mud and rain. Robots are most likely to concentrate on picking fussy crops that can't be dug up by machines—peppers, tea leaves, and fruits, for example. Scientists in Israel and Italy have already tested robot tomato-pickers, with great success.

Halt! Who Goes There? ....

Many businesses, museums, and art galleries in the future will be thankful for their robot security staff. Robots won't fall asleep on the job or get distracted from their task of constantly patrolling the building, seeking out burglars. If they encounter an intruder, they will film the person and sound an alarm. Some security robots may be equipped with water cannons or tear gas, or a special sticky foam that hardens in seconds and prevents a person from escaping.

In the future, people will use home robots as part-time security guards, mobile fire alarms, and housekeepers. Robots might also take to the streets as shop assistants or traffic monitors. As soon as robots go public, though, some people will have worries.

The answer to all three questions is that we're not completely certain. A robot could be programmed to operate safely and be tamper-proof in virtually every situation. If it encountered something it didn't understand, a robot out on the street would err on the side of caution—it would not do anything harmful. If it sensed a problem with one of its parts or felt someone trying to open or damage it in some way, it could be designed to shut itself down. The problems are likely to be with people rather than with the robots themselves.

Spaced Out ....

Away from the public and out in space, there's no doubt that the importance of robots will increase. There are already plans for robots to refuel satellites, and for robot maintenance workers on the International Space Station. The farther into space a mission goes, the greater the need for machines, which don't need huge supplies of air, food, or water. Any colony on the moon or Mars will probably start with dozens, possibly hundreds, of robots to build living quarters and other parts of the space colony before the people arrive.

A Million Robots in a Glass...................

One possibility for the distant future is that we might build nanobots. What are they? Well, imagine the smallest possible machine you can think of—then shrink it, and shrink it some more.

Nanobots are robots that are so small they're measured in nanometers, which are billionths of a meter, or about the length of ten atoms. Researchers have already made some very simple devices of this size. If nanobots are built in large numbers, life will never be the same. They could fight disease, clean our teeth and blood vessels, clear up pollution, and even repair holes in the ozone layer.

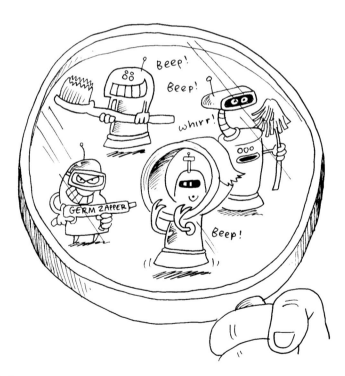

Long before nanobots arrive, there will be intelligent, versatile robots at home and at work. Now that you have an idea of what's involved, maybe you'll grow up to be the proud owner of a robot or two—or even a whole family!